1

Buried by the Ocean
Stolen by the Moon

Grayson Wyatt

INTRODUCTION

Don't be afraid to reinvent yourself. Through invention, we find what we never knew existed. When we don't challenge the constraints of our habitable world, we become just another piece of the backdrop, an everyday item taken for granted. Don't take yourself or your dreams for granted; both wait for your fullest attention. Once delivered, you will become more than you could possibly imagine.

Mother, Lover, Defender

The wonder of light,
the miracle of sound,
the wisdom of the wind,
the world all around.

I feel your presence,
surround my soul.
It speaks clearly to me,
It guides me home.

Your love is a wonder,
And a blessing bestowed.
The gift of life—
Wrapped in a passionate glow.

continued -

The sound of your voice
Brings my heart to rest.
Like the wonder of your love—
Brighter than the rest.

The wisdom in your touch,
Soothes the wildest of beasts.
You are all that is wonder-
The world trusts in thee.

The future we dream—
Only you can see.
Without your loving spirit,
None of this would be.

So, carry the flame,
And keep up the fight.
You are a mother, lover,
And defender of the light.

fin.

A Future Not Yet Told

In your scent, I lay
As we bask in the sun
With morning rising
Your touch is still fresh in my tingling mind

Touching just minutes past
Your scent is warm
And in your soil
I plant the seeds of an unknown future

Tarot cards read the future cannot be seen,
but just as hands of a clock long to cross
in time our souls will be lost

Hearts that walk among the dead, with little feet and
wonder for all. Like books that must be read
those last few moments before bed

The joy of this world is so very often hid
But through the eyes of the new
The map can lead

continued -

Worlds of the past need let go
Your future is unclear
But your soul has a glow
As you grow in warmth and lost emotion
You will be a mother full of devotion

Walk this earth as though you own it
You are all that it's made of, and for that, you deserve it

You are a woman, mother, and lover.
People's worst enemy and sometimes all that's left to wonder
You are one with all, you have become a mother
So walk this earth and share with the other
The confusion and wonder
That it is to be a mother

fin.

Just One Sip

We've no health, and the air is thin.
It's been weeks now, to no end–
floating around in this endless drink.
Windless, stuck, lost at sea.

With the sun beating down, and the supplies running low.
I feel a mutiny on the horizon– a tension starts to grow.

The crew grows weak; I'm afraid their minds are amiss.
A few of them have jumped ship– to sink into their abyss.

Like lions, we scream and roar.
Fighting our minds while dreaming
of shore.

The ships gone crazy, it's just a matter of time–one
by one, we're falling behind.

continued -

With rations gone, several days past.
There is no friend, only the dark future –running out fast.

A single taste, or just a sip.
I dream of food and think, what if.

Just one sip to wipe this look from my face,
One taste to end it all.
A sip of lead, followed by a puff of smoke,
Will send me- free my cares and all.

fin.

Whisper in the night woods

In the Silence of still:
I hear the world just outside

Its wild, free, and green-
Just like me on the inside.

So I come to this place
to seek the unknown.

Not from your world;
but instead from my own.

A place of voice
Internal and true.

Where all things are real-
Nothing untrue.

This place I seek, with my back to the ground,
feels like home- I feel the love all around.

Grayson Wyatt

fin.

You are Deep Sea

When he comes
You'll never know it was your turn.

You'll only see a flash
Of light--and bubbles of concern.

No friend can save you now:
No matter how close the tether-
or level of pal.

You're on your own with time ticking fast.
He has come to take you: Into your deep crevasse.

As the light fades and your heart starts to slow-
You'll pass into that world, so few of us know.

Go deep into your dreams: I'll see you on the other side.

You are my brother, together we will be,
Rest at ease my friend- You are deep sea.

fin.

Grayson Wyatt

LSD

On the corner of time, I can hear

Beats rhythmic with rhyme.

Pump after pump-

Never a straight line

Like the mad hatter running with my mind:
This beat drives me crazy with every second of time.

Forget yourself and places you know
We're taking a trip;
A trip to the unknown.

continued -

The far side of the moon
From just a tiny drop- sends my heart racing,
Like a run-away clock.

Shadows that dance
On waves of pure sound: this madness is temporary,
But I can't come down.

Gone from this world on a planet far away.

I'm looking at myself - from a hole in my brain.

fin.

Grayson Wyatt

Carrier of Light

What is in- comes out: what is out- comes in.

It all depends on your mindset
and power within.

Don't be so quick to hand out your key-
You must protect your light; from those who can't see.

With the light inside you; and darkness all around
Keep walking the path; keep your eyes to the ground.

The clues are small and difficult to read-
so pay attention closely, or you might not see.

The choice is the path; if only you believe:

continued -

The path you choose is the one you can achieve.

To bridge this gap, and show the world your light-
You must strengthen yourself,
Be ready to fight.

It all depends on your mindset and power within,
what goes out: must come in.

So receive and accept the universal flow-
It's the fuel for your light, and garden for your soul.

Walk with faith and love in your heart;
Because a carrier of the light-- is never alone in the dark.

fin.

Return to the land

When your thoughts
are heavy, and they
won't unwind.

Take a walk in the
woods, and leave
it all behind.

It's here you'll know—
that calm voice—deep inside.

This is you; working
out the problem
from the other side.

continued -

As fears wash away
like the babbling brook.

So does your concern
and heavy look.

As each moment passes
she's holding your
hand.

Helping you forgive, forget,
and return to the land.

fin.

Untitled

People Speak of Love
like it is rose'
picked daily from a
garden of no compromise;
where everyone
flourishes.

But love is quite obtuse,
the opposite of
what's described
to you.

Love is veggies and
fruit and all piled in
a heap.

It's your job to sort
what to throw,
and what to eat.

fin.

Holding

I've often wondered.

How long I could hold
flame.

The burning ember—
gray ash and pain.

Each time I try, it
hurts a little less.

After all these years—
I've only come to

find.

It's the pain I love,
not the flame—
deep down inside.

fin.

Daughters

Wherever you walk,
I walk with you.

Through hardships and trials—
straight lines and jagged.

Wherever you go,
I wait for you.
Your return, slow—
like seasons passing.

However, your journey—

regardless of time.
I am your father,
In my heart you are mine.

continued -

So see the world,

and journey where you must.

You can carry me with you --in spirit

just trust.
A wild, free girl: wonderful and bright.

I still sit with you
on the coldest of nights.

fin.

THE WALLS THAT WE BUILD

The walls that we build,
are tall and strong.
They stand as though nothing can ever cross.

Brick by brick we stack ourselves high,
so that no matter how tall--
you'll never see the other side.

Great walls of rock and mortar

held together with fear and pride.

Do we even know why we build these walls
down deep inside?

If we stand next to our wall,
do you suppose we can hear it fall?

continued -

Or will the wind of time and pain keep it
through heavy trial and strain.

The ground which our wall stands--
is solid and strong.

We should build better on such things, so we could look inside
or climb to the top.
Instead of standing behind our walls talking of what's
over there and continuing to mock.

If I had more brick -I'd build a sidewalk,
or maybe a half wall- so people could walk to it
and admire the crumbling of pride on grief-stricken soil

fin.

Grayson Wyatt

Quietly Alone

Have you ever wondered
what it takes to be
alone?
To walk the hard miles;
with no one there to cheer you on.

Have you ever wondered what it's like?
To fight the hard fight—
night after night.

Have you ever felt
like you couldn't go on?
Only to wake—
to another dawn.

Then you know what it means,
and this thing I speak of.

continued -

To look within—
and rise above,
to believe in yourself
and learn to love.

Through all the storms
and endless nights.

Those darkened hours
give us worldly insight.

Its when were alone
and hardest hit;
we truly see ourselves—
and mustn't quit.

So, fight your fight, alone
and un cheered -struggle
through the darkness
even if no one can hear.

fin.

Grayson Wyatt

My Overboard

My breath takes me—

a thousand bees sting
at once.

My heart begins to race.

A sense of calm—
I've never known.

Floating in dark;
looking up at the
stars.

continued -

My breath is all around.

Cold, and calm.
I slip to the
other side.

My watery grave
I have found.

fin.

Vision

I watched you smile in my dreams.
I looked around and realized—I had died.
Your smile radiated of want and warmth.
But I was on the other side.
I looked around, and it soon became clear.
You weren't smiling at me—it was him my dear.
Turning—accepting the light,
I walked away from the love of my life.
They say if you let it go, and it returns—
It was meant to be.
What to be said—when she walks away,
No longer smiling at me?

fin.

Two Paths

Two feet.
Two Miles.
Two Beds.
Two people -living their own lives,
in their heads.
Two kids; that pass the time.
Two lives apart from mine.
Too many reasons to list
for all the times,
I've dreamed of your two lips.
To you -I say, goodbye.
Too many reasons -I can't say why.

fin.

ANCESTORS

Walk into the world—
don't be afraid.

You're not made of glass,
crystal, or clay.

You can handle some wind,
rain, and snow.

It's deep down inside there.
Don't you know?

continued -

You're made of those things-
that came before.

Survival and hardships,
nights on the floor.

So, look within, and the lessons you know.
It's deep down inside there-
don't you know?

fin.

Mother Ocrean

I can feel the stones
under my feet.

The smell of the ocean
and the taste of the sea.

The wind at my face—
with the world behind me.

I'm drawn to this
place—every
time.

Holding my hands—
you take my cares
away.

I look into your
sunset; and
hear you quietly say.

continued -

Come to my shore
and your energy
I will heal.

You are a child of this
Earth—my love
you can feel.

Waves of wisdom
wash over my feet.

Taking with them—
all that's worrying me.

With ease of breath,
I let it all go.

Standing in your wonderful current—
your amazing glow.

fin.

ME AND FIRE

Silence

Just beyond my
world—all is black.

Around the fire- I
dance with glee.

Naked, alone, free.

Me.

fin.

The Day You Walked

There was a day
when we use to walk.
There was a day
when we use to talk.
There was a day
when I knew your soul.
I could feel which direction;
you wanted to grow.
There was a day
I could no longer see.
The person you were
or who you wanted me to be.
The day I knew it wasn't me-
the day you walked away from me.
The day we talked- you told me why.
I sat down alone and cried.
A seed from he; not from me- the reason we will never be.

fin.

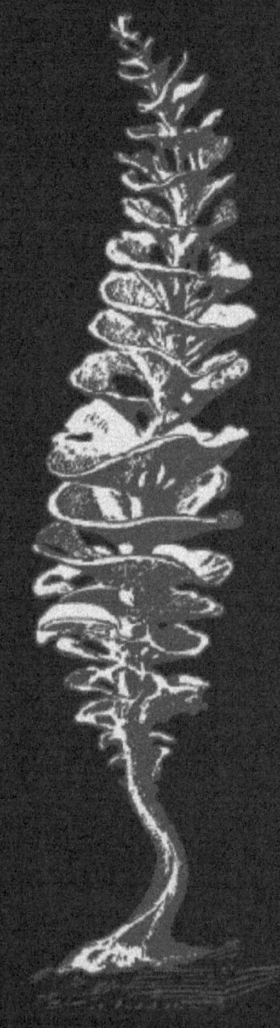

Grayson Wyatt

Like A Book On A Shelf

I once read a book

It reminded me of you

Page after page I read until the meaning was true

I still love that book

I can see the words- like gloss

I read it's title from afar

Because I am afraid of it's- loss

fin.

Grayson Wyatt

The Passing of Seasons: Shedding

Tiny leaves falling down.

Spinning, spiraling, fluttering
around.

Red, yellow, brown, and gold.

A delight to my eyes;
a warming of my soul

the sign, we're here-
for another round.

It's been a hard year-
nose to the ground.

continued -

Let it all fade, and flutter
away—all these hardships
of yesterday.

The season is now, and your
time is short.

so, shed your leaves-
begin again.

Winter is here, like
a long-lost friend.

fin.

Out of my Head

There are writings
here and there.

Some I've lost-
others I don't
care to share.

They're jammed in books and
tucked away.

Some lost forever-
to my dark eternal flame.

continued -

I'll keep writing
and spilling it
with lead.

It's all I know,
the only way
I've got.

To get it all-
our of my
head.

And untie the
knot.

fin.

THAT GUY

I awoke this
morning

searching through
the trash

I threw my
life away
again

in the moment
of collide, just
me, myself, and I.

continued -

The meeting
of want, anger,
and pride.

Crumbled and tossed.

Me-I'm left
to sigh.

Once again
I'm that guy.

fin.

48

Thoughts of You

I slid into you,
in my dreams.

I awoke this morning-
to find you still
on my mind.

I stepped inside, and
walked around a
bit.

continued -

Still loving what
I find.

Your memories and
thoughts, let me
mingle about.

Relaxing this worried mind.

The image of you-
always brings me
to calm

and soothes this heavy mind.

fin.

Brothers

Two heads of brown

scruffy, messy-all
around.

Cowlicks galore-
wild and free.

Walking behind—
now I see.

What it is to be a
brother.

continued -

Stand, walk, fight,
and love the
other.

Like shadows that
twist and tangle.

They merge as one-
with wild splendor.

A feeling combined and
amplified by 10.

It's the love for a brother
-something you can't pretend.

fin.

Dirt, Rock, Crud

All the things
I love

give me a shovel
and watch me
go

I'll dig to hell

and tell the
devil

NO

fin.

Childhood On A River

Stones in a creek always make me smile
They remind me of childhood
A time that was free- and wild
Just like a stone sinks with ease
I too joined my solid brethren
In the water with ease
Type after type
So many colors to see
The water was home
A place I longed to be

fin.

Dead Sisters

I knew your smile,
I knew your face.

I called you sister
my heart; you held a place.

One day there; and
suddenly gone.

My heart sank,
I carried on.

I found you again;
many years past.

Only to find, that
moment had passed.

continued -

Different in way, nature
and sound.

I see your heart-
hard, cold, - a fighting ground.

What I remember of
you; and what you turned out to be.

They look different
in my mind; and how it should be.

You were mine,
and I was yours.

Sister & Brother
till the end.

You died all those years ago;
and today once again.

fin.

Spill It With A Pen

Beautiful white paper
Lines clean and crisp
I wonder what shall become
Of this emotion laid by a pen
I put it down lick after lick
Trying not to drown
These words I spill
Are just the things in my mind
The life I've lived
The one I'm trying to find

fin.

To The Sea, We Went

Aboard we went for fortune and fame
The world's bounty-ours to claim
Through darken seas and freezing nights
We sail our souls in endless flight
Treasures are few
Hard times holdfast
Living on this ship
Sucks sailor ass

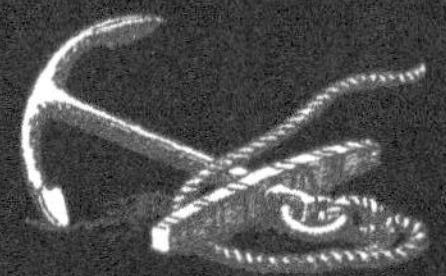

Cowboying: All The Things I Miss

Stables of wood worn by weather
Smells that remind me of home and leather
Long talks next to a friend
The campfire our prize in the end
Morning mist, through the rain, fog, and all-
I learned nature summer, winter, and fall
The long rides-when you can think and let it all go
The arrival at home
Your spirit a glow

fin.

Stepping Over

I remember the day I died
Water black-clean white tile
I still remember his smile, looking down,

Patting my soul
Thankfully, I awoke from his nightmare
Just him washing my hair
From the water, I was born again
By the hands of a dark, dark, man

fin.

The Un-Spoken Moment

I can still remember her silhouette

Lines smooth, gently curving
A slight bend of her head catches my attention
I can't stop wondering
What's the image in her mind?
As her finger curls away, brown
Hair on tip
It keeps me falling, stumbling, thinking what if?

continued -

This place of wonder, I explore deep in my mind
Is driven by passion
Something I can't fight, or, care to hide
Finger twisting I'm lost in her vail
Slight curves gently flowing
I can see the answer there, just past her eyes
Our souls fight but resist to stay inside
Silhouettes now emerge soaked in sweat
I no longer wonder what she is saying with those eyes
I felt her, and she felt me
This is the way we came to be.

fin.

Early Seasons, Into Hard Weather

Winters past we spent loving each other
wrapped in a blanket of understanding and care.
As we grew in our winter slumber, our hearts became one;
we started to share.
Springs arrival let us shine,
and give our love to one another,
completely divine.
Together we planned, planned for a future so bright.

continued -

The seed was growing, only a matter of time.
Our life together became our goal
and united we rose to raise these wonderful souls.
As parents, we stand united for the greater good.
Our differences aside, we both understood.
To do it, and do it right,
it will take all we have; it will be a fight.
The love of two boys will carry us through.
Not just the hard times, but the unknown too.
I hold your hand through this my wife,
the best story ever written;
the story of our life.

fin.

Mother Earth

Desert, woods, forest, or jungle
She goes by many names
I know her as mother
From the prairies of the west to the mountains of the north
From the waters of her oceans
To the driest reaches of her desserts
I lovingly embrace my mother- she holds my hands

Blessed was I- to walk among her fields
She showed me, guided me, blessing me with skills
A life lived, walking this earth,
I look forward to going back to her soil
If I'm so deserved
To begin again and start a new
Let my body nourish you

fin.

It's not about approval, or, the money I can earn
It's about seeing what I can become
Regardless of concern
To be me in the fullest sense, walk a walk, worth walking
Say I gave it my best

The book they read long after I'm dead
Will mean much more than money
When they no longer hear the sound of my voice
Speaking of vinegar and honey
Read my words once again re-connect
With your father, follower, and friend
I write for you my sons
Until the end

fin.

Believe It First

When that time comes -and it comes to us all
Stand your place -even if your back's against the wall
Just take a breath
Look deep down inside
Hold on to the thought; I can, if only I try
The fear that cripples
Can Empower instead
If only you paint that image,
First in your head

fin.

Watching From Behind- Morning TV

I watch a zombie from behind
He's small and blue- around the age of five.

The house is on fire, and bodies are everywhere.
Cotton as far as the eye can see.

He's tired now, sitting in a gaze-
The stuffed toys; a memory haze.

With treat of gold, I temp to sway-
Honey, chips, chocolate gay.
Nothing works, I'm sad to say.

He's lost in another electric haze.

fin.

SECOND CHANCE

Something happens on the other side
The clock stops where your soul resides
Standing in front, so many souls, all around
I'm looking at my clock, sitting there, on the ground
They're concerned, and so am I, my second hand stopped
I'm not sure why
Encouragement from peering souls, wanting my spot,
To move forward and go
Start it they say-some start to yell
We all have the choice
It's this or hell

continued -

Thousands of voices all interject
To move forward-I must learn how to accept, forgive, and forget
This is my clock to start if I will
This time move forward with grace and skill
Standing in front, I kneel to the ground
Softly touched my second hand-awoke and found
The dream of my life had been my past
After you killed me
I was given a second chance

fin.

In the Wind

I live in the wind like a flower
Dependent on your love- they're scattered showers
Only you can let the sun in
Yet, the curtains you close
Wind battered and ragged- I still wait for your love

fin.

In the Mind

To be in the mind
Is to fall under one's scrutiny 24/7
An exhausting endeavor

fin.

Scrap Words

74

Scribble as you care
It could mean something-someday, somewhere
A thought from the pen is like a dream in wake
A gift given
Don't forsake

fin.

Untitled

The voices you hear are one in the same
One speaks from wisdom- the other from pain
Follow the voice your heart knows to be true
It's the voice guiding you straight to your deepest desires
Pushing you through

fin.

Grayson Wyatt

The Moon and I

Fire just outside my tent door
I can see the shadows bouncing wall to floor
Alone on the peak looking down
A spirit on perch listening for a sound
Quit, calm, and still

My soul becomes one with your will
Together the moon and I
Calmly sit with a quiet mind
Shadows reflecting memories I've left behind
The moon-a portal to the other side

fin.

Born of a Tree

My inner cells are talking with my outer cells
My outer cells are calling them home
To the woods, I shall go
Home

fin.

FIVE SHORT POEMS

To say I love you
Is to condemn you.

If these titles place us on the shelf
Leave me un-finished

We know not the chapter
In which we appear in someone else's novel

Watch your performance closely
The world is
Perform like you want to be picked
And the universe will

It's the principle pursuit of
my endeavors-
Family

fin.

WRITTEN

I would rather be written well
A story of this magnitude takes time
There might be mistakes
But in the end
It will be as it was meant to be written

fin.

Two Short Poems

My human body
Can't keep up
With my god-like mind

I remembered what it felt like to hold you
Just before I died
I died smiling

fin.

Shame

Yesterday you where hurt- I was to blame
Today I walk around covered in shame
My hurt was deep and greater still
Not from the words I spoke
But the way I feel

fin.

Dreaming of One

I heard a voice in the middle of the night
It was your soul inviting me to flight
We danced on the clouds and visited the stars
I awoke in the middle to find you laying where you are
A dream so real it made me ask
Who is this soul?
Why the distance so vast?
My soul longs to fly with yours and dance among the stars
For now, my dreams will have to do
Your sleeping, dreaming of someone different, someone new

continued -

Our souls aren't together I'm watching you
Your smile and sounds of glee
Sadly reveal, your flying with someone- it's not me
With sadden soul, I sink back in bed-
Quietly wondering in my head
Where have you gone, who you are with
Our souls are so apart- yet here I sit
At the end of it all, before I close my eyes
I release my soul from your bind- your forgotten heart
The promise you made is no longer true
So, fly with your other
Let your souls dance as one

I'll always remember you
You were my one

fin.

The Coffin

I'm ready to rest- today they put me in the ground
In a soft bed with pillows all around
This bed is quite cozy trust me when I say
Never has seven feet been so roomy
It's a house of wood with handles to go
I even have a door in case it starts to snow
There's no widows- but I'm sure I won't need one anyway,
My blinds are safely secure
I can't see my feet or touch my toes

continued -

Bending is overrated where I'm about to go
My nose is itching so but for some damn reason,
My finger just won't go
I'm starting to cramp, and the air is getting stuffy
I've noticed a funny smell- I wonder if something is rotting
So here I lay, needing a haircut, with no place to go
I would rather be in hell, than in this room, all alone
I've looked, and tried, to no avail
I still can't find the light switch in this tiny cell

fin.

PART II

RELEASE

When you finally release me
I will find the love
That's been waiting for me

fin.

My First

The noise outside brought me to rise-
Startled, scared, nervous inside

I stepped out, flashlight in hand

I remember the sound-
The stillness of the night

With two steps he emerged

I pulled my gun and yelled down-
or your dead

Failure to move-
And fear for the worst

I shot him dead

Killed my first

fin.

Grayson Wyatt

Young Again

Little boys run around-
Crazy and wild

I wish I was a kid again-
Maybe I could smile

The dreams they share-
Light my day

Reminding me of a time-
I wasn't so gray

I see them scream and flail about-
Like wild Indians on the chase

When I awake from this dream-
I'll be ten again

This time win the race

fin.

Walking through Fog

A misty glow is cast about, it's hard to see-
I'm full of doubt

Stumbling forward, I try not to fall

The fog is so thick-
it's like a blinding wall

Everything's wet and it's as cold as ice

I'm not sure where I'm going-
Or what it means when I arrive

I keep walking on faith-
Something I hold deep inside

I must get through the fog-
Somehow find the other side

To reach a place I've never been, seen, or heard

Joy, money, happiness-
All the things I deserve

A world constructed by me

The only ones allowed-
Are those that love me

fin.

Moving on

Death, is but one step-
The easiest in fact

It's the reward you earn-
After you complete your task

Leaving the party is never fun

But, when its over-
Its over

Time to move on

fin.

The Rhythm of You

Sometimes I wake up-
And watch you sleep

I turn and face you-
And listen to you breathe

Quietly in and out, with a steady flow-
you're so peaceful, in that place you go

I focus and calmly get in rhythm-
And become one with your beat

Like standing on the oceans shore-
Your steady rhythm calms me

Falling in sync with you-
It brings my heart and mind to a quiet place

Not long after, I'm falling asleep-
Looking at your beautiful face

fin.

Dreams

The dreams I have are driven by desire-
A longing for more

Not in some sense of dirty pleasures-
Just for the sake of wanting more

No, their much more than that,
and they're held deep inside

It's the fulfillment of what drives me,
something pushing me from the other side.

continued -

To be loved, wanted, and desired at all cost-
with a smile cast my way

Not because I asked for it, paid the bills, or
guided in some way

But because you couldn't resist me-
No matter what I did, or could possibly say

Like a tree longing for light-
It doesn't know why

It just keeps reaching for the sun-
hoping to touch the sky

fin.

Such is life

We often fall

This is the nature of life

Pick yourself back up and begin again

It's how we cope with the fall and deal with the stress

That shows the world what were really made of-
The grit we possess

Don't let a fall cripple you from your dreams

Stand up and say I can

Get a running start and try once again.

What have you got to lose?

Falling is part of life- embrace your bruise

fin.

Wild Thing

Clearness of self only comes-
in the absence of light

It's when the world is darkest-
I can finally see with clear sight

The eternal fire-
deep in my soul

Hoping the darkness shows the other side

Like a wild thing-
waiting to rove

I sit in quiet glee-
waiting for the show

fin.

THE EMPTY SOUL

There's a hole that leads to nowhere

Massive and wide, so deep nothing comes out

It swallows the light, along with everything you might throw in it

At the bottom of this pit, this darkened abyss-
There's a pile stacked high

Of all those things, people, and dreams
I've thrown to the bottom-deep inside

I stand at the edge with my wagon piled high

Item after item, person after person-
I've cast them down inside

Somehow, I thought it might reach the top-
So, then I could see

continued -

Everything that piles made of, all those dreams I've thrown in-
That I thought could never be

There is still no sign, or glimmer of hope-
They're lost in my dark abyss

I now understand-
It slowly becomes clear

Each item tossed; every dream cast within-
with every person I've lost

Took a piece of my soul as they were tossed

Wagon empty-with a hollow heart

I cast the last person in-
To make it all stop

When will I reach the bottom?
This I do not know

I'm in free fall now-
Empty, hollow, without a soul

fin.

Grayson Wyatt

End days

Chop, chop, goes the bone-
Splinters, screams, and moans

Your plea's will not save you

I'm hungry and all the world-
Has gone to hell

One after another, I feast

Bodies consumed. I'm pleased

I the good man of my past-
Was killed long ago

Regret for the dead-
I do not show

I've become one-
This I know

With the keeper of death-
His gruesome show

Grayson Wyatt

fin.

Messages From God

You can read them in the day-
Or even at night

He sends them all the time

O-it's not the way you think-
It's a bit more divine

Just look in the sky, trees, and rocks-
Its written all around you

Messages from God are in nature

He's trying to remind you

fin.

Soul Mates

We have been with each other through many lives-
Together we have lived and died

Our hands know the other-
Through the love we both shared

We keep coming back to each other-
With warmth and care

I walk with you now-
Like I walked with you then

A guiding light, a long-lost friend

continued -

My soul is tethered to yours-
With a bond stronger than time

You keep coming back to me-
And I to you

Because we still had lessons to learn-
Our connection is eternal and true, regardless of time

Be it this life or the next-
I'll always be with you

fin.

THE WEB OF LIFE

I watch from a distance-
At the web I have spun

Forty-two now, the web is vast-
And reaches halfway across the U.S.

Lives set into motion-
Actions that can't be re-lived

Broken hearts, little feet, crushed dreams-
It's all in there

They hang around like the days catch-
Waiting to be consumed

continued -

If they only knew, they have the power-
to free themselves

There doesn't have to be doom

But they don't

They just hang around-
waiting for someone to save them

No one will

fin.

One Thought

If I had but one thought to impress upon people-
It would be this

Children are a gift to be enjoyed in the fullest-
They're here for only a brief time

Just as a man is only a man once-
And a child twice

A child only radiates of wonder for so long-
It's ever fleeting

One day the world will get ahold of them-
Just as it did you

fin.

Words

If I wrote two hundred poems and only two you liked

I've won at expressing myself-
Showed you what's inside

It doesn't matter if they all approve

It's what I bring to my table that reveals my higher self

Read my words, sometimes with discontent

Somewhere deep down-
You understand what is meant

fin.

FAMILY

I love my family-
Heart complete

My two little boys-
With their quick little feet

A wife that's asleep-
Warm by their side

112

I go forward in this world-
So, I might provide

A life only dreamed of-
Words fall short

I hope to give them all those things-
Their dreams are made of

fin.

Lessons

The many lives and people-
I've experienced along the way

Where angels sent to light-
And guide my way

Whether through pain, love, or abuse

They all played a hand at pushing me through

fin.

AFTERWORD

Adventure

At every corner,
there is amazement
waiting to be found.

My heart could never
sit still or be one with itself.
It could hear only the beating
of the drums from those corners
of the world not yet discovered.

Like my elders before,
I will continue exploring new shores
and sailing those lines
I have not yet sored.

fin.

Buried by the Ocean Stolen by the Moon

Publisher Contact:
hi@saintmemory.com

www.saintmemory.com

If you have any issues with quality, delivery, or content and would like to report it directly to the publisher, please visit feedback.saintmemory.com.

Printed in the United States of America for distribution worldwide.

CPSIA information can be obtained
at www.ICGtesting.com
Printed in the USA
LVHW010710130122
708375LV00010B/781

9 781087 987323